Stay Safe

THE OPERATIONS MANAGEMENT GUIDE FOR ACTIVE SHOOTER THREATS

How to Approach Business Operations in the Age of Increased Mass Shootings and Other Random Acts of Violence

written by Cornell Rogers

CONTENTS

PREFACE

I walked up to the BBQ restaurant and surveyed the layout. It had an open patio dining section that faces the street. The area has newly built apartments, multiple restaurants, and a few bars; it is a lively area during lunch hours and on weekends. I thought to myself, *this is my ideal customer. The restaurant is in a square that has high foot traffic (an ideal target for an attack). Plus, a shooting in a restaurant just happened three days ago... If there is a business owner that recognizes the need for security protocols, it is definitely this one.*

I asked an employee if the business owner was available; he said yes as he pointed to him. I stood by as I waited for him to finish serving his patrons. When he finished, he came to me and asked, "Hey, what you got?" I showed him the manual and asked, "What plan does your business have in place in the event of an active shooter situation?"

"Run like hell."

I oftentimes have trouble maintaining my demeanor, so when I heard this, I'm sure he saw the look of bewilderment come across my face. I looked him in the eye waiting for him to say that was a joke and give me a real answer. But he was serious.

I went to another business, but this time it was the office of an engineering company. I walked in and was greeted by the receptionist. I told her I worked in building security and that I wanted to speak with someone in management. She walked into the first office nearest her desk. While I waited in the lobby area I surveyed the place for security, specifically, what could stop someone from carrying out a mass shooting if they were standing where I was. Their security was non-existent. The front of the building was all glass, and I could see the employees walking around inside. I could enter the front door at will. Then once inside, everyone was easily accessible should one have the determination to reach them and cause harm.

A few moments later, a member of management came out shaking her head 'no' as she asked me, "Can I help you with something?" As I introduced myself and began to speak with her about building security, she continued to shake her head 'no' the entire time. Then she eventually cut me off saying, "No thanks, we don't need anything."

In my experience, I knew that this engineering company had the same emergency plan in place as the BBQ restaurant – in the event something happens, *run like hell.*

INTRODUCTION

Due to lax gun control laws and the recent uptick in mass shootings, every organization should have a plan in place in the event of an active shooter situation; a plan that goes a little more in-depth than just *'run like hell.'* According to *Gun Violence Archive*, the number of **mass shootings** (defined as 'a shooting where four or more people are shot or killed, not including the gunman') that have occurred over the past few years are staggering:

- 2014: 270 mass shootings
- 2015: 335 mass shootings
- 2016: 382 mass shootings
- 2017: 346 mass shootings.

As of September 23, 2018, there have been 264 mass shootings. September 23 is the 265th day of the year. That averages out to one per day. Please note: these *are not the number of victims* of mass shootings; these are the *numbers of times* a mass shooting has occurred.

It is the responsibility of the organization's leadership to have a means of ensuring the safety of those that come to their facility or event. This plan should not be a one-time deal: each time the doors of the facility are open, or an event is being held, there needs to be a clear emergency plan that has been well-communicated to those present. Anything less than this is pure negligence, considering how the recent surge in mass shootings has reaffirmed to us the harsh reality that an event like this is increasingly possible.

Another harsh reality that is associated with an active shooter situation is the fact that you cannot count on police to save the day, primarily due to the time factor. The average active shooter situation lasts **12.5 minutes** – the average emergency responders' time to an active shooter situation is **18 minutes**. That means the gunman, if carrying one semiautomatic weapon, will have the time to get off dozens of shots and then safely flee the scene before law enforcement arrives (which we have seen in most instances). If the gunman is using an automatic weapon, he will have the time to get off a countless number of shots. 12.5 minutes is an *eternity* if you are in a situation where you are unarmed, yet you are hiding or fleeing from someone who is armed, while you wait 18 long minutes for law enforcement to arrive.

This manual will help you get a plan in place for your organization. What you will find listed here are general suggestions based on the common layouts of most buildings and outdoor events. If you would like a consultation on how to design a plan that is specific to your building or venue, contact Palm Resources Group.

THE GUN DEBATE

The right to open/conceal carry firearms is a subject of hot debate. This manual is not endorsed by the National Rifle Association, nor does Palm Resources Group have a pro-gun agenda. If you are one who is against carrying firearms, your belief and opinion is respectable. However, you must consider the threat posed by the growing number of people who own them. It is now easier than ever for everyone to legally purchase firearms, including those who have malicious intentions. And if you manage an organization or host events, you **must** consider this question: *if a gunman opened fire at your facility (or venue), how is your organization prepared to respond to protect its employees and customers?*

No one who has been in this situation, who was unprepared to respond with force, ever thought it would happen to them – until it happened. Those who were prepared emerged as heroes who stopped villains on a rampage. When guns are used properly (e.g., in an active shooter situation), they can significantly reduce casualties that would otherwise occur.

SECTION 1.1: SECURITY PROTOCOLS

The times we live in demand a change in your approach to leadership, with the need to implement security protocols being more important. The days of leaving multiple entrances to a facility unlocked are gone. The days of entrusting everyone's safety into the hands of an off-duty cop are gone. The days of not having to worry about something like this happening are gone. Active shooter situations should be on your emergency-situations list, alongside fire, severe weather, earthquake, etc. It is now necessary for you to have an emergency plan in place in the event someone walks in the front door and opens fire.

Although those in management are aware of the frequency of mass shootings, many have put very little thought into contingency planning. Upon hearing of shootings in settings like the ones they work in, they usually do not make any changes or take precautionary measures. They do not have any emergency plans written nor have they communicated anything to their staff. Their plan is usually only as thorough as imagining what they would do in the situation: *If that happened here, I would try to fight the gunman... I would run to the car and get my firearm...*

Simply thinking about what you would do is not enough. You need a thorough plan of action on paper that consists of:
- Knowing the layout of your facility or venue and securing it
- Identifying, evaluating, and training personnel with the means to stand guard
- Creating and communicating a plan of emergency.

Covering these three bases will give your organization the security protocols it needs. But without a clear set of security protocols, your place of business is a sitting duck.

SECTION 1.2: SECURING THE FACILITY

The first step in creating security protocols is knowing the layout of the building. How many entrances are there? Are there any entries that a gunman could access without being spotted by security? If it is an outdoor event, securing the venue is even more challenging. You must think like the gunman would: *what areas in this setting could be used as vantage points for an attack?* Then you must ask, *is there a way to minimize the number of potential vantage points*?

The solution is to control all entries. The fewer entrances you use, the better. You need to keep all doors that lead to the outside inaccessible except the ones that are guarded. If you limit the number of entrances to the number guarded by security, the gunman will have to go past security before carrying out an attack. If the venue is outdoors, security needs to be strategically placed in locations that are optimal vantage points for an attack. Remember: you must think like a gunman. In the second section, we will cover how to train security to recognize potential threats and effectively guard their territories.

Here is a diagram of an organization in a small building. This could be a bank, restaurant, doctor's office, etc. The circles represent people. The red circle is the gunman, the black circles are security, and the blue circles are everyone else. The blue rectangles are entrance/exit doors.

DIAGRAM 1

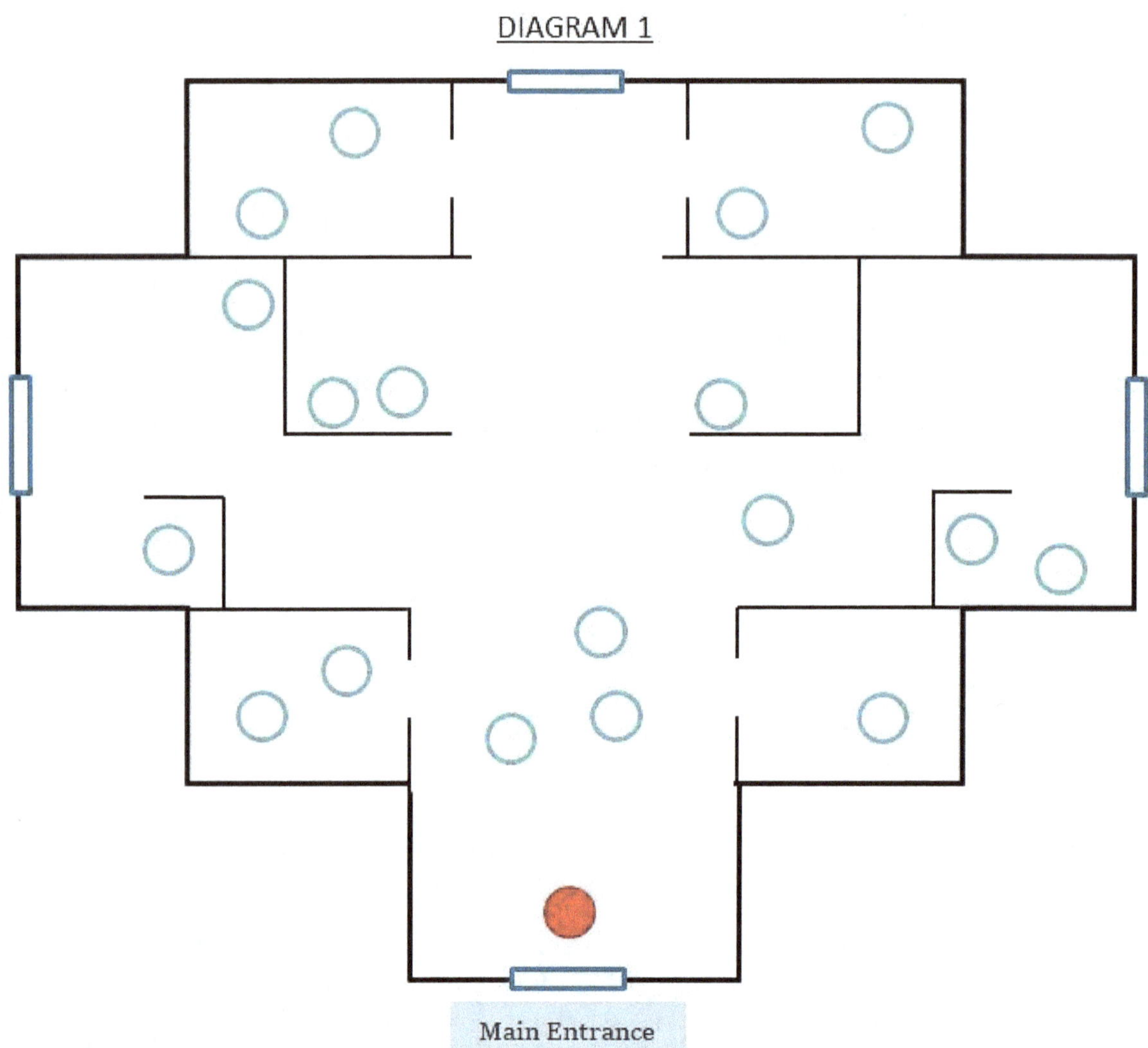

This is what it looks like when there is no emergency plan nor armed personnel. Everyone will run to the nearest exit or attempt to hide when the gunman opens fire. And in this situation, you will encounter the maximum number of casualties.

To secure this facility, there needs to be a guard near the entrance. Now the use of the term 'guard' in this manual does not always carry the implication of a hired security guard or police officer. A guard can be anyone within your organization who is licensed to carry and trained to use a firearm. The investment of having people within the organization trained to respond in a situation like this is invaluable.

There is a drawback to having a uniformed security guard or police officer at the entrance: your first line of defense will be the gunman's first target if he is committed to carrying out his attack. Remember: you must think like the gunman would. *If you planned to carry out a malicious attack, and you saw someone in uniform at the entrance, would you attack him first?* Yes. In fact, if you saw a police vehicle parked at the building or venue, it would help you better carry out the attack. You would know that there is an officer present, so you would modify your plan by locating him and then carrying out your attack in another part of the building (because it would take him a longer time to find you) or simply attacking him first.

The solution is simple: have a guard – whether that person be security, police, or trained personnel – dress in plain clothes and to conceal carry. Then position them near the entrance(s). This will give you the upper hand on a potential threat. The gunman will not know there is a guard present. When he unveils his weapon, the guard can neutralize him as quickly as possible, resulting in zero to minimal casualties. Here is a diagram of how that would look in the same building as Diagram 1.

DIAGRAM 2

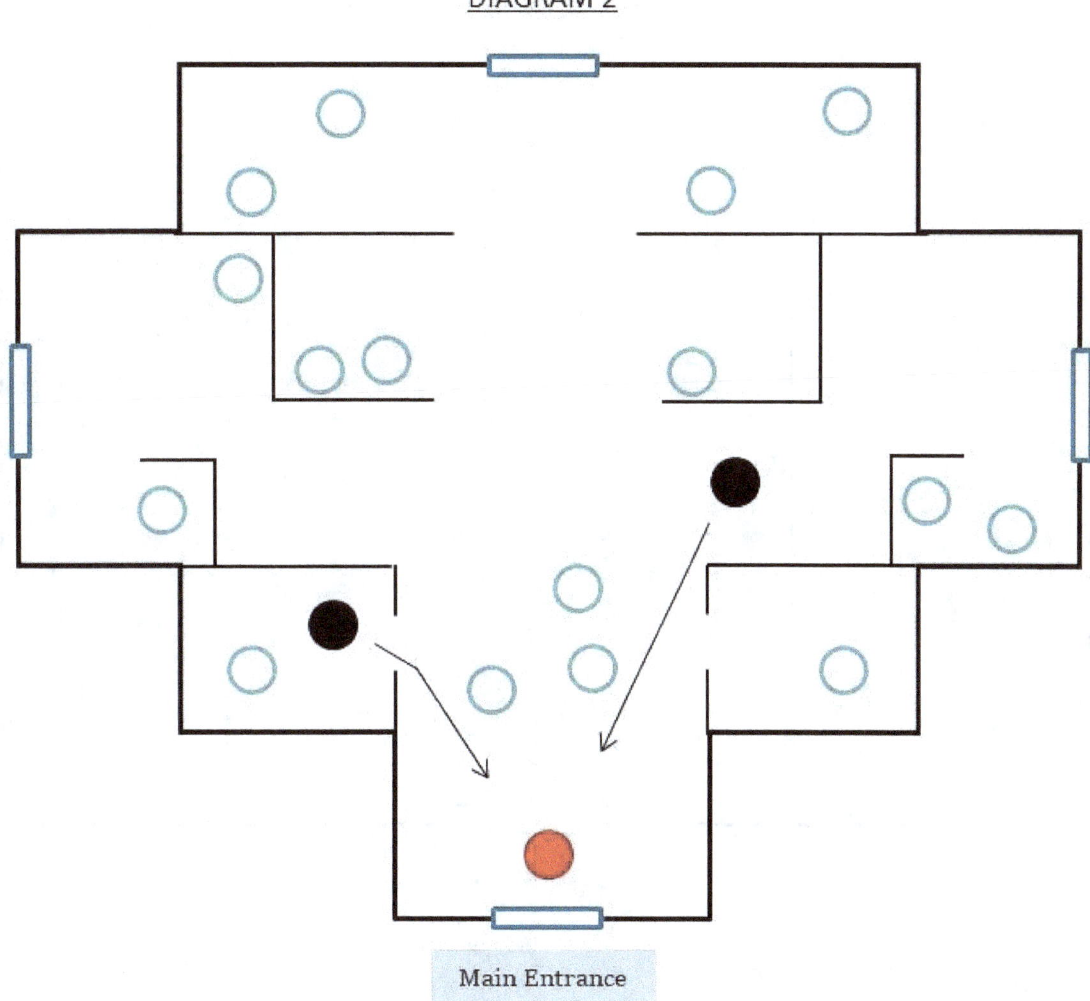

Here is a diagram of a building with occupants, for example a place of worship. Most of these have the same layout: a large assembly in one part of the building, and smaller groups in other parts of the building. Again, this is what it looks like when there is no emergency plan nor armed personnel. Everyone will run to the nearest exit or attempt to hide when the gunman opens fire. And in this situation, you will encounter the maximum number of casualties.

DIAGRAM 3

Another safety concern that is common with sanctuaries is the number of doors that are unlocked and unmanned during times of assembly. This is not the case with any other building (whether public or private – think school, restaurant, bank, store, office, etc.), but when it comes to religious settings, the doors are usually open and unmanned.

The first step in securing any facility is to limit the number of entrances to the number you can effectively guard. All doors that lead to the outside that cannot be guarded, should be kept locked and used as emergency exits only.

The second step is to strategically place armed guards throughout the building. Several factors will come into play as you strategize where to place them, such as: the number of people who attend, the size of the building, the number of small groups that are meeting outside of the main group (e.g., nursery, teens, women, etc.). The layout of the building in Diagram 3 reflects this. To ensure maximum security, guards need to be placed at the entrance(s), within the main assembly, and near each small group meeting area. This reduces the response time of the guards (ensuring they get to the gunman faster) and gives them a clearer view of the threat, reducing the risk of striking a bystander. If you only have one guard at the main entrance, and the gunman starts shooting in a different part of the building, the response time will be slower as the guard would have to go throughout the building looking for the gunman. And by placing multiple guards within the large assembly, the closest one to the gunman will have the clearest shot; if you only have one guard and the gunman is across the room, his shot will be much harder if people are panicking and the gunman is mobile.

In the fourth section of this manual, we will cover how to train customers and visitors on what to do in the event of an active shooter situation, so it will not become a scene of pandemonium.

See Diagram 4 for an example of where to place guards within the facility.

DIAGRAM 4

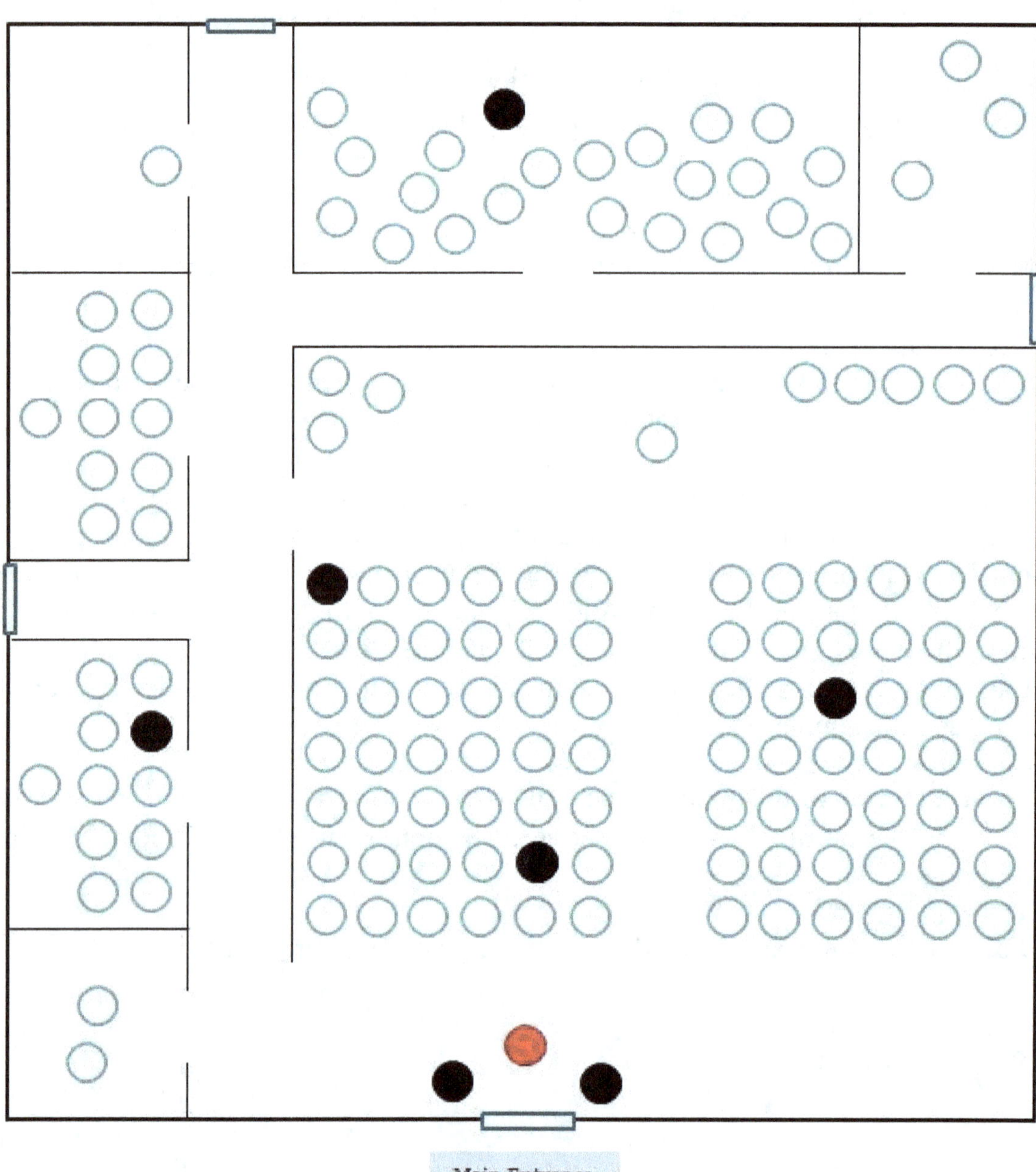

This is an ideal setup, not an exact pattern to be followed. Depending on how many people gather at your facility, you may need more or fewer guards. How you choose to set it up is at your discretion. Just remember the main objectives when doing so, which are:
- To break down the total area of the building into smaller territories
- To position a guard in each territory
- To give the guards a clear line of sight at any possible spot within their territory.

In addition to the placement of guards, you need to secure the grounds as people enter and leave in large numbers. At worship services there is usually a bottleneck flow of people arriving at the beginning, and a reverse bottleneck flow of people leaving afterwards. You should strategically place guards in good vantage points outside of the building to guard the people as they arrive and enter the building, and back on their posts as they exit the building and leave the premises.

For a consultation on designing a plan that is right for your facility, contact Palm Resources Group.

Here are diagrams of an outdoor event (e.g., concert or wedding). These are more difficult to secure due to the number of vantage points, as represented in Diagrams 5.1-5.5 which show the gunman in different places. The additional symbols are a street, bushes/trees, and blue rectangles for cars. With no emergency plan, everyone will run away from the direction they believe the gunfire originated and it will be complete pandemonium.

DIAGRAM 5.1

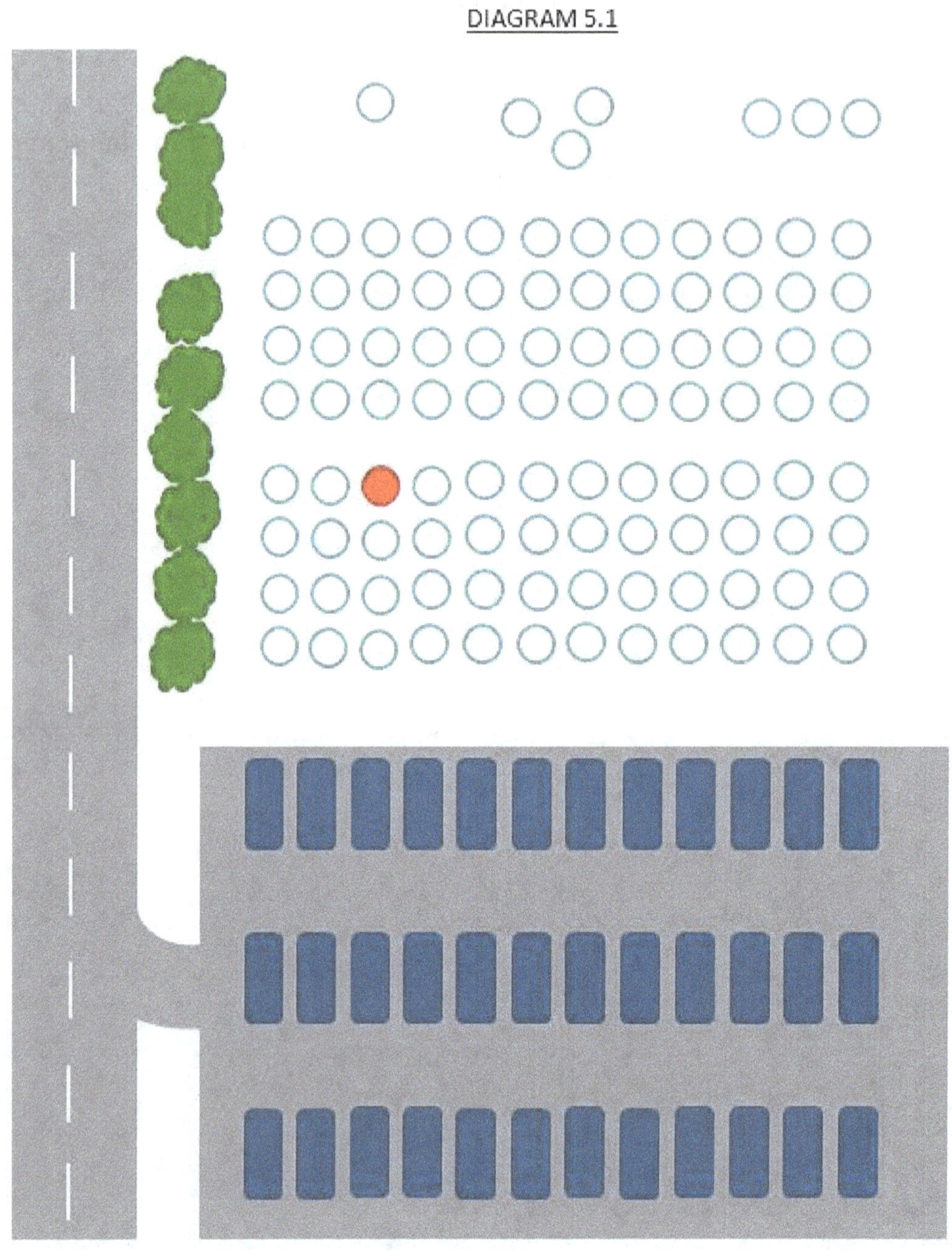

DIAGRAM 5.2

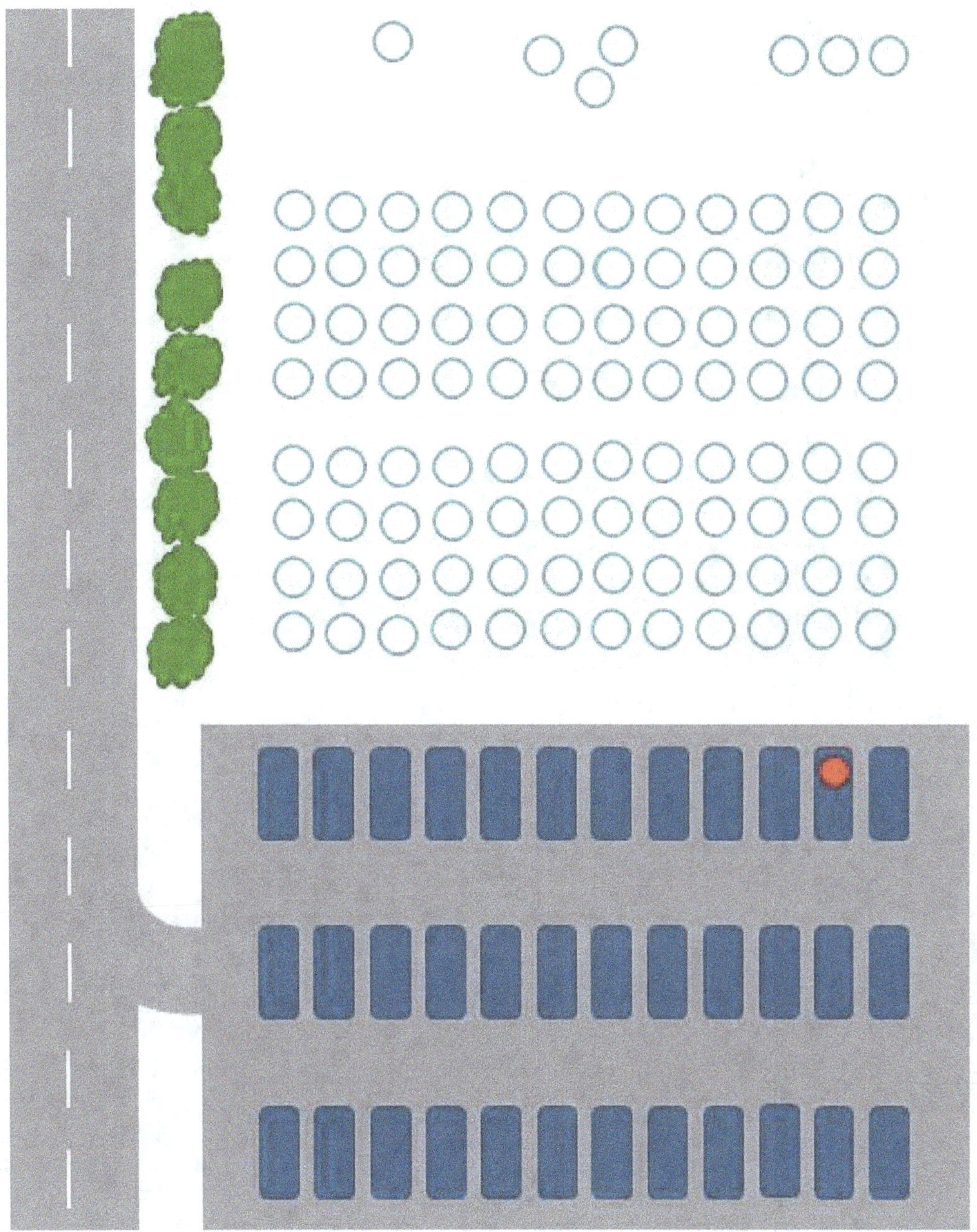

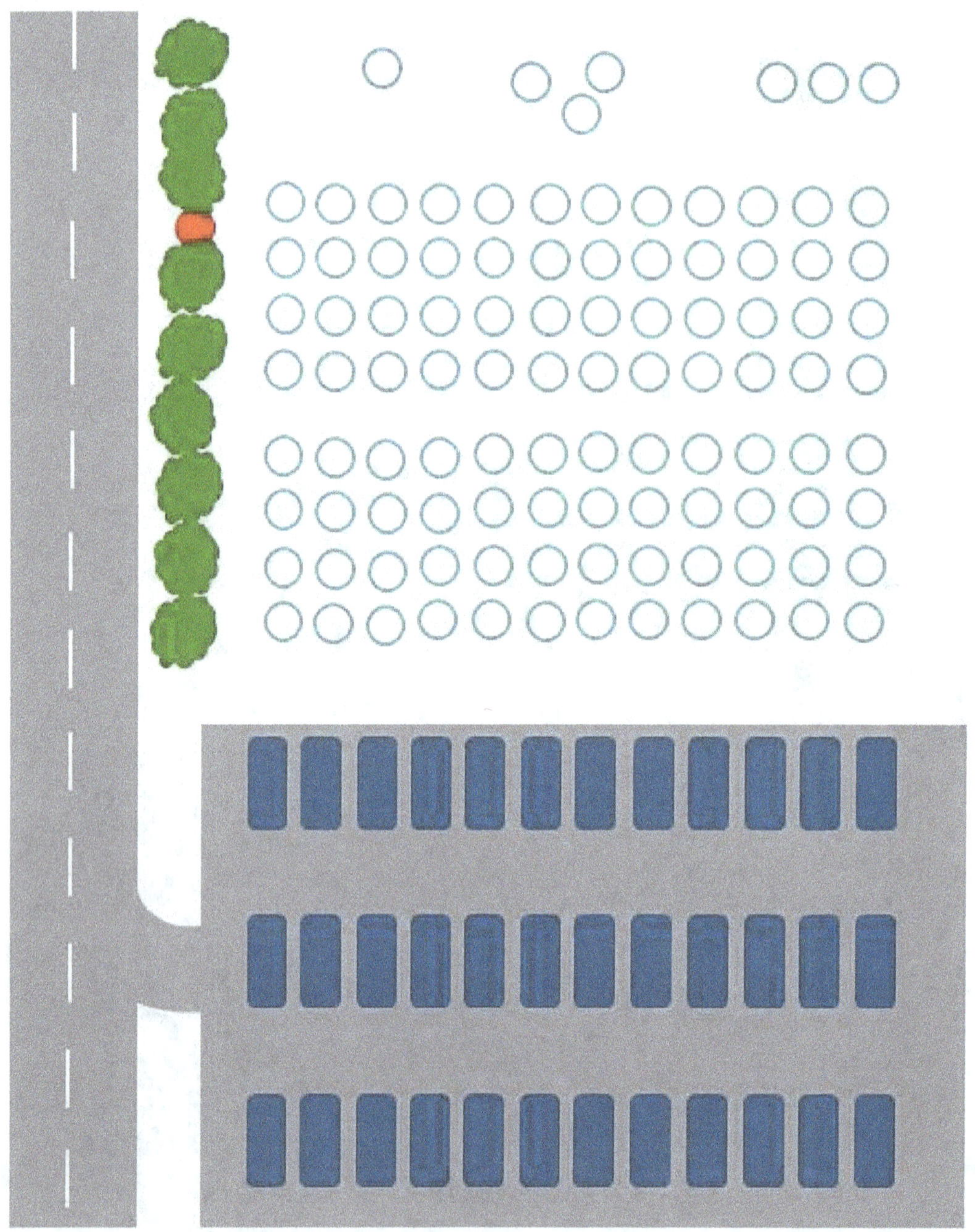

DIAGRAM 5.3

DIAGRAM 5.4

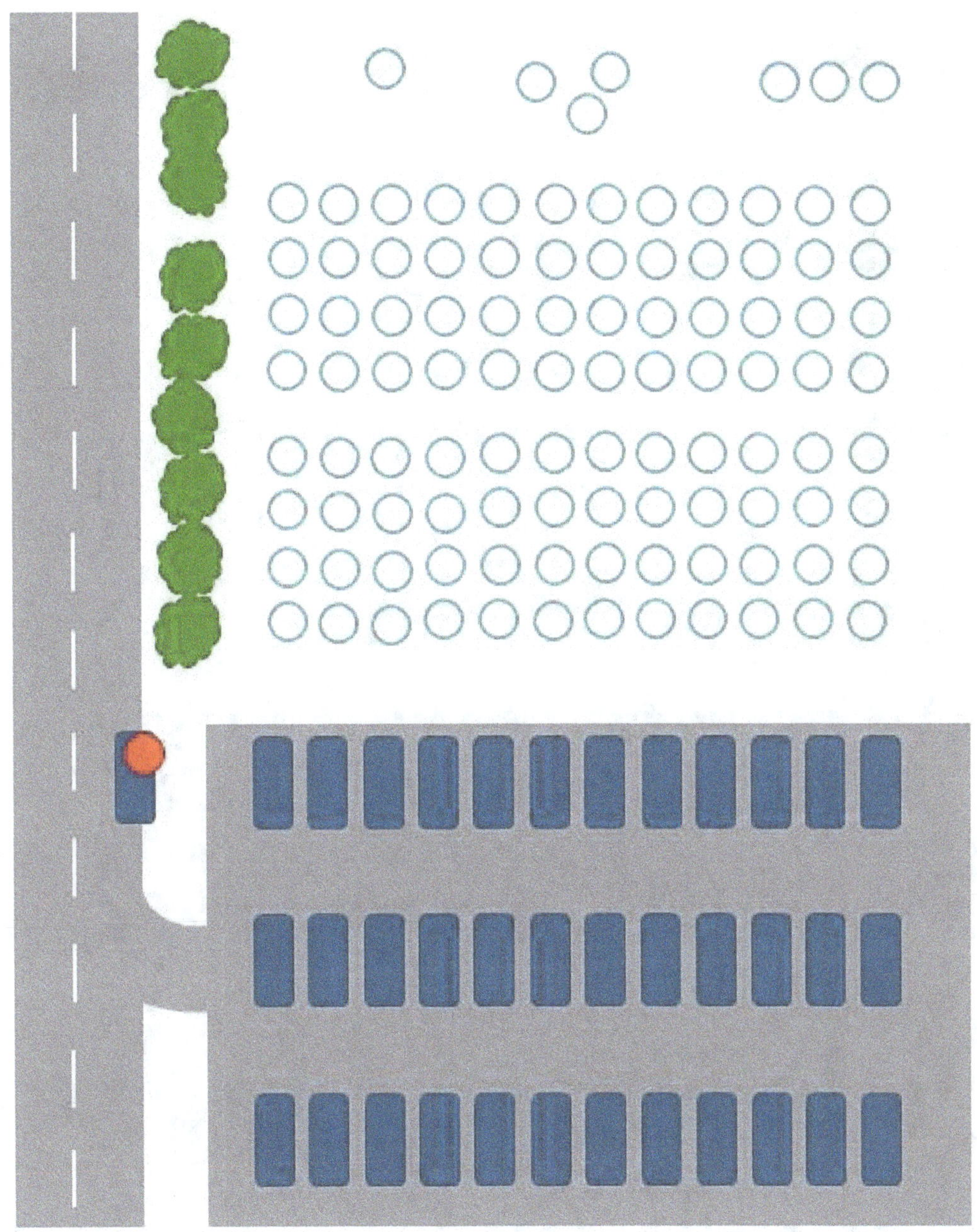

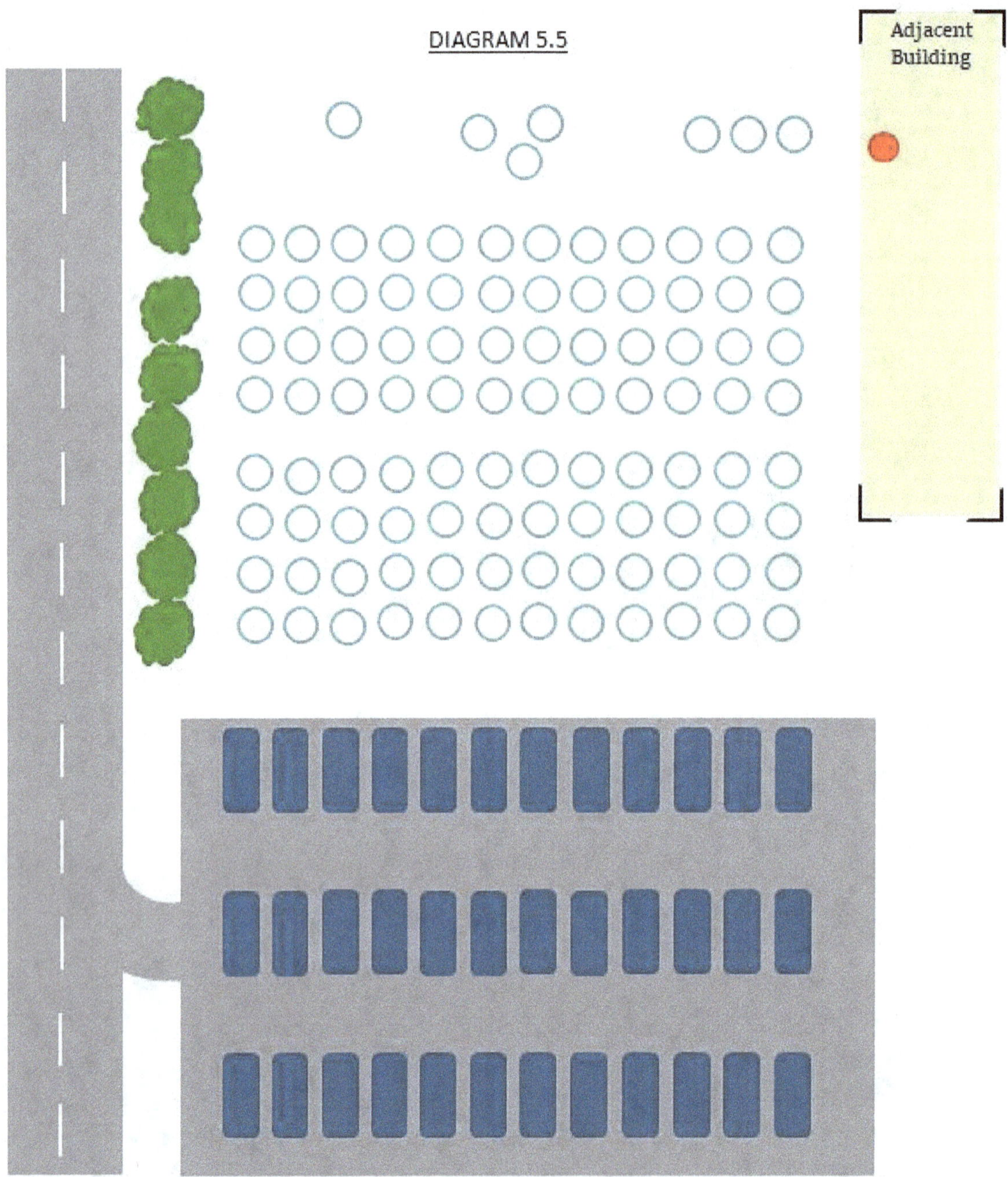

As you plan outdoor events, you must budget and implement additional security measures to ensure everyone's safety. There needs to be a guard at every potential vantage point, including the parking lot and adjacent structures (e.g., the Las Vegas gunman was in a nearby building). There also needs to be a single point of entry so all attendees can be checked upon entry. You can create barriers to entry by renting a gate and placing it where needed.

Diagram 6 shows how an outdoor event should look with proper security measures. The yellow line represents a gate.

DIAGRAM 6

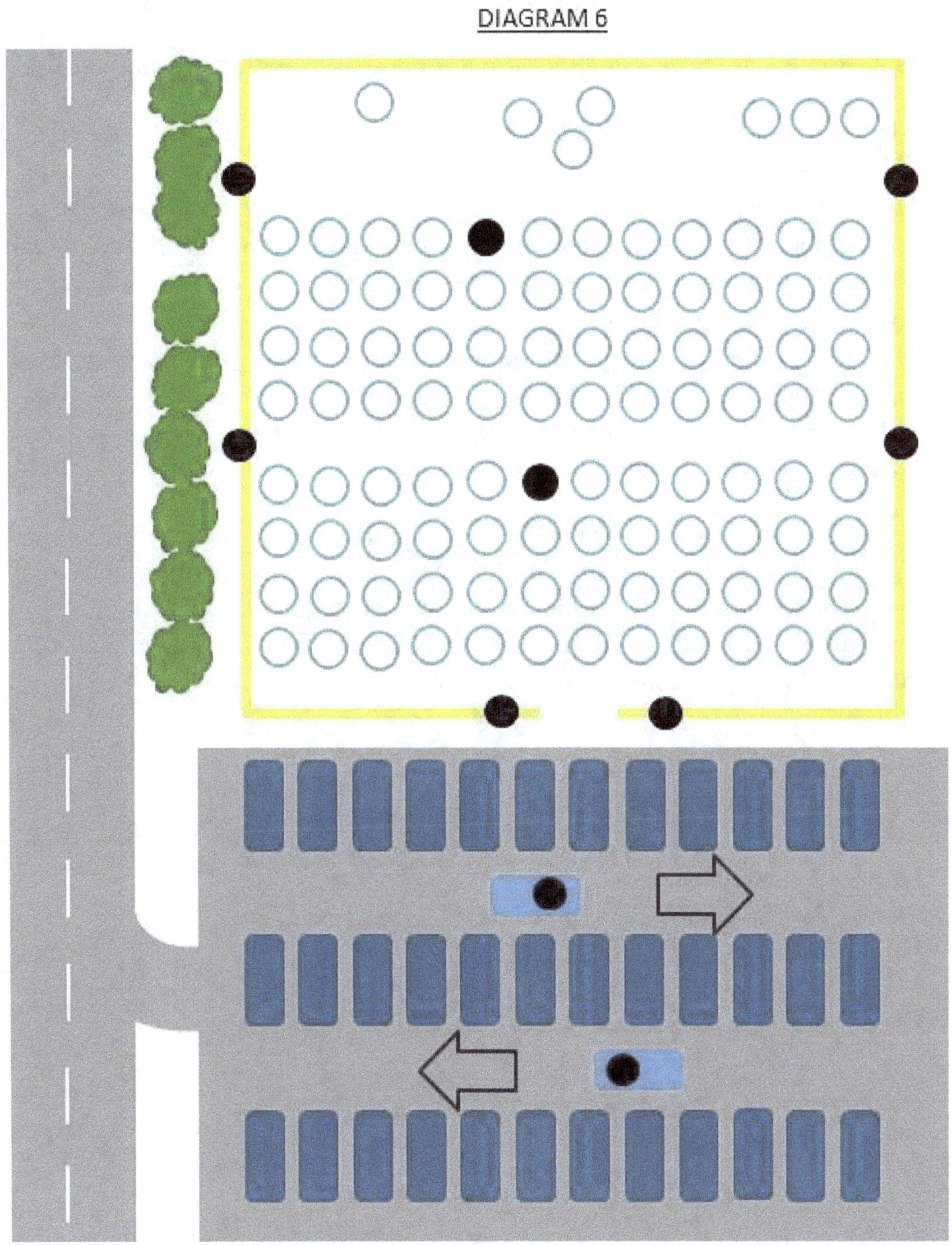

Just think: *how many events have you attended that did not have security checking for weapons?* You and everyone else who was present at these events were at high risk.

When security is being planned, oftentimes those in management have two stigmas that hinder them from implementing sufficient security protocols: they are concerned that it will offend customers/attendees, and that it will be too time consuming and costly.

However, you must look at the examples of management in industries where the day-to-day operations involve high security measures, such as airports and sporting events. Those who fly *appreciate* the sense of security they have knowing the other passengers were checked for weapons. Those who attend major league sporting events *appreciate* the sense of security they have knowing the other attendees were checked for weapons. Consider the standards of security in these industries and ask yourself questions such as:

- *What tactics are these organizations using that my organization can take and implement on a micro level?*
- *What security measures work for them, and what are some they need to change?*
- *How can I provide the highest level of security in a timely, cost-efficient manner?*

They have also educated their customer base on what to expect – no one thinks twice about having to go through security to board an airplane or to get into a sporting event. It has been that way for so long that everyone has become accustomed to it. Although you may have some initial pushback, within a very short period of time your customer base/attendees will grow accustomed to your new security protocols.

SECTION 2.1: IDENTIFYING GUARDS

The second step in creating security protocols is selecting personnel to be guards. Make no mistake about it: you need guards present whenever the facility is open and there are occupants. The dilemma is your organization may not have the resources to have an off-duty police officer or armed security guard present each day during operating hours. If your organization has the resources, you should invest it without hesitation. And as previously stated the most effective approach is to have them dress in plain clothes and conceal carry.

However, for the organizations that do not have the resources, there is still a way to get the same level of security – promote from within. Take an inventory check of your personnel: who within your organization has served in the armed forces or worked in law enforcement? Those are your top picks. They have already been trained in the areas necessary for the role, that being *firearm safety* and *active shooter response.*

If none of your personnel were in the armed forces or have law enforcement experience, the second-best option is to identify those who are willing and have the aptitude to be a guard. Note: this does not require that they leave their current position. For a small incentive (perks on the job, a slight pay increase, etc.) the right candidate will be more than happy to take on this additional role.

These people are also easily identifiable; in fact, you may have already talked to them and seen their ability to be a guard without noticing it before now. Ask yourself:
- *Who within the organization is always talking about their gun collection?*
- *Who is known for carrying a firearm on their person when they are not at work?*
- *Who is known to for keeping a firearm in their vehicle in case of emergency?*
- *Who is wary of visitors in the building while others are customer-focused?*

Your answers to these questions will give you the best candidates for fulfilling the role of guard. These people have a protective nature. In fact, if you allowed it, they would probably take on the role free of charge. But by paying them or having some other incentives, you will maintain control and ensure they follow the guidelines you put in place.

Before empowering these individuals, we recommend:
- A background check
- A time of close observation (unbeknownst to them)
- Firearm safety and active shooter response training
- Establishing clear guidelines for the role (i.e., to guard against attacks, not act as sheriff).

A genuinely protective person will thrive in this position. Whatever job perks or pay increase you couple with this new role will make it even more attractive to the right candidate.

Please note: you should not attempt to recruit for this role. It requires the person to place themselves in danger, which is not their original purpose for becoming a part of your organization. If you do not have anyone who is willing to take on the role, shelve it for the time being. And as you make hiring decisions in the future, keep in mind how a person with armed forces or law enforcement experience could benefit the organization in more than one way.

SECTION 2.2: TRAINING GUARDS

After identifying guards, you need to establish their operating procedures. The level of security you want to implement is at your discretion. *Do you want everyone who enters the building/venue to pass through metal detectors? Do you want everyone to be searched using a handheld metal detector? Do you want to allow everyone to enter freely, but only subject those wearing heavy coats and clothes that could be used for concealing to be searched?*

These are important questions you will have to answer. Regardless of what method you use, there are two key points you need to remember, and those are *consistency* and *recognizing a potential threat.*

Oftentimes, security protocols are inconsistently enforced. Police and security guards tend to pay closer attention to people of color (i.e., of African American and Hispanic decent). It is your responsibility to make sure that the guards understand that the protocols are in place to prevent a mass shooting, and not to serve as a policy of prejudice. Inconsistent practices will result in a bad customer experience that could severely damage your organization's reputation. Consistency is the key: whatever measures you implement, make sure they are implemented equally across the board.

In connection with the point made above, you must know how to recognize a potential threat. You should research "mass shootings" and carefully examine the scenarios in which they happened, and the people who carried them out. There is a reoccurring theme you will find: they were mostly done by individuals who showed warning signs prior to their attack; and when they attacked, they were dressed in such a way to conceal their weapons. After looking at pictures of them, and hearing statements from those who knew them, you will see that most of them gave off frighteningly strange vibes. We tend to gravitate toward things that are concrete; however, being able to pick up on more abstract things such as bad vibes, odd behavior, or a look of madness in one's eyes, could be the difference between life and death. Those who are a part of your organization should be watched more carefully if their behavior or demeanor changes in a negative way. If they are not someone you see on a regular basis, but rather a customer or visitor, look for the warning signs: *does this person appear visibly distraught or anxious? Are they wearing an excessively large shirt or long coat that could possibly conceal weapons? Have they had a bad experience with the organization or with their co-workers in the past that could have set them on edge?* ***Do they have any unnatural, awkward bulges on their person that appear out of place and are not in the shape of a common object, such as a cellphone?***

Your guards need to be on the lookout for all of these warning signs.

As we look at the example of the church shooting in Charleston, all the warning signs were present before the act took place. Dylann Roof, a Caucasian teenager, entered a predominately African-American church during a time when they do not normally have visitors. The survivors recalled that he sat there quietly, intently, for ***over an hour*** before making his move. Racial profiling is wrong; however, some people in some situations cannot afford to be overlooked. The difference between a negative profiling experience and a positive encounter with security is all in the approach.

Police are trained to be <u>tactically civil</u>. That means being courteous to everyone yet prepared to subdue anyone who poses a threat. Your guards need to adopt that same approach: they must be kind to customers and co-workers while being prepared to use force at any point and time against any of them if they pose a threat. Someone entering the facility or venue who is wearing an excessively large shirt or coat, carrying a case/bag that does not fit the occasion, or has a demeanor that raises hair – those are red flags you cannot ignore! The guards should immediately engage that person. Their approach should include:
- A kind greeting
- Bringing them into a secluded place (so as not to create a scene)
- An explanation of why they were stopped
- And searching them using a handheld metal detector or a pat down | asking them to remove their coat or open their case/bag to show the contents of it.

If they have an ulterior motive, you just saved the day. If they did not, then thank them for their cooperation and understanding.

Due to the frequency of mass shootings and lax gun control laws, everyone recognizes the need for greater security protocols. This preventive measure you take should not turn away customers/visitors if done correctly (we recommend having a second guard present in these instances for accountability and safety). And anyone who is against basic security protocols that ensure everyone's safety is probably not the type of person you want at your place of business or worship. Do not allow the few who will push back to dissuade you from implementing protocols that protect the whole.

SECTION 3: LETHAL V. NON-LETHAL FORCE

The most important part of establishing security protocols is choosing the right personnel as guards. The second most important is determining what level of force the guards will be able to employ; specifically, lethal versus non-lethal.

In high stress situations, tasks need to be simplified. If the goal is to stop a gunman on a rampage (the peak of high stress situations), then using lethal force, i.e., a firearm, would be the most effective. The guard only has one task: to aim and fire. Once struck, the threat is neutralized, and no further action is required on behalf of the guard.

The drawback to employing lethal force is the risk of striking someone other than the gunman by accident. This risk can be significantly mitigated by having the guards attend a firearm safety course and spend time practicing at a local gun range. However, this risk will always remain if a firearm is involved.

The other option is non-lethal force, or properly known as *less-lethal weapons*. There are a variety of less lethal weapons on the market that are available for purchase. These include stun guns, tasers, pistols that shoot rubber bullets and bean bags, etc. The obvious benefit of employing less-lethal weapons is the risk of fatally striking the wrong person has now been erased. These weapons temporarily incapacitate the target, which is beneficial if needed in a setting where the gunman could be in the midst of people running frantically.

The drawback to less-lethal weapons is the incapacitation is only temporary, meaning the threat will be reactivated after he recovers from being struck. The guards will have to move in quickly and attempt to disarm the threat before he recovers. This can be very dangerous, as they would be approaching an armed threat that could recover at any moment and begin shooting again. Also, there is no guarantee that the less-lethal weapon will incapacitate the threat. In the event it does not, the threat will likely be agitated by the pain and become more determined to finish his assault.

This decision is one that you and your leadership team will have to consider as you implement security measures. It is not an easy choice between the two, but it is better to have something than nothing at all. Being completely defenseless in the face of a gunman is far worse than the risks of employing lethal or less-lethal weapons.

SECTION 4: COMMUNICATING THE PLAN

The final step in establishing security protocols is creating a clear plan of emergency. You must sit down with your leadership team and have a candid conversation: *In the event someone walks in and opens fire, what are we going to do? Should everyone attempt to escape using the nearest exit? Or should we take cover while the guards neutralize the threat? What will we do if there is more than one gunman present? Will running to the nearest exit be the best solution if there is a second gunman elsewhere?*

Although this scenario is an uncomfortable topic to discuss, you must come to grips with the serious possibility that it could happen at your facility or event, and you need to have a plan of action in place in case it does. For a consultation on designing an emergency plan that is right for your organization or event, contact Palm Resources Group.

Once you have a plan in place, the next step is communicating it to staff. Everyone who works in your organization needs to know the plan and practice it. They will be able to guide those who do not. If you work in a facility that has a minimal number of non-employees who visit, this is as far as your plan needs to go.

If your facility has high foot traffic of non-employees, or if you lead a religious organization where most of the people present are not a part of your staff, you must come up with a way to communicate your plan to them. Again, we can look at the examples of how this is handled by organizations in industries that have a proven record of success. The one you will find most relevant is that of airlines. The last thing any person who is flying wants to think about is their plane crashing. However, at the beginning of each flight you receive explicit details of what the pilot and flight crew will do and instructions on what you should do in the event of an emergency. The pilot explains that he will land at the nearest runway or bring the plane down on a body of water, and that you are to fasten your seatbelt and put on your oxygen mask. No one is detoured from traveling when they hear the captain say these things.

What can you take away from their example? At the beginning of <u>each</u> meeting or event you host, you should tactfully cover your emergency plan:

"Thanks for joining us! We hope you have a good time. In the event of an emergency, we ask that you use the exit located nearest you. You can find them (exit A location), (exit B location), and (exit C location). Thank you!"

"In the event of an emergency, we have undercover guards in place throughout the building for your protection. We ask that you do not attempt to run as it may cause confusion and

hinder the guards from having a clear view of the threat. Rather, we ask that you lie on the floor and take cover until the threat is neutralized. Thank you!"

Communicating a plan of safety should cause those present to feel safe, not turn them away. This may also detour an attack. Remember, you have to think like the gunman would: *If you planned to carry out an attack on a group of unsuspecting people, and then found out they have a good, tactically responsive plan in place for such occasions, you would feel as though your plan had been thwarted and you wouldn't want to continue with it.*

If the nature of your business makes communicating your plan to non-employees impossible or impractical, you need a well-orchestrated plan in place that will work despite the unpredictable factors that will arise. These include, but are not limited to:
- People running, resulting in a large chaotic scene where it is hard to find the gunman in the crowd
- People running and getting in the way of the guards, resulting in them not having a clear shot at the gunman
- Someone who is not a guard yet has a firearm, who attempts to bring the gunman down (which will confuse the guards on who's who)
- Someone who is not a guard attempting to physically take the gunman down, resulting in the guards not having a clear shot.

You must secure people who are unaware of what to do in the event something pops off. Your measures of security should include limiting the number of entrances, setting up metal detectors at the entrances, and having undercover guards in place. They should practice different scenarios, so they will be better prepared to respond to a situation should one arise.

CONCLUSION

We know that as a manager of an organization, your goal is to find ways to cut costs and maximize profits. So, the idea of investing in security to safeguard from a situation that might not seem likely may not sound appealing. But you must remember: 'not likely' and 'not possible' are vastly different. Although it is not highly likely it will happen, it is a very real possibility that it *could* happen. Keep in mind that no one who has been in these situations thought it would happen to them. And given the recent uptick in these occurrences, you cannot afford to not take precautions. **If something were to happen, you could be held liable in part and heavily, publicly criticized for your failure to implement precautionary measures.** And, like all organizations that have experienced an attack, you will react with costly, over-the-top security measures; but by then it will be too late. Therefore, we recommend that you do not allow the costs of implementing security protocols to hinder you. Be proactive: make the investment!

TRAINING SERVICES

Our mission is to equip your organization with the tools you need in the event of an active shooter situation. We offer two services: ***security plan design*** and ***self-defense training***. Our security plans are designed to safely evacuate persons based on the unique layout of their facility and the location of the threat (gunman) within it. These plans also include the identifying of safe zones within the facility if evacuation is not an option. Our self-defense training, **H.H.C.G.**, is based on military and police tactics. We go hands-on when training your staff to effectively strike, subdue, disarm and neutralize a threat.

For a consultation on active shooter response training, contact Palm Resources Group by email at info@palmresourcesgroup.com.